ROBERT MAASS

When Summer Comes

Henry Holt and Company · New York

This book is dedicated
to a summer in North Branch.

Library of Congress Cataloging-in-Publication Data
Maass, Robert.
When summer comes / by Robert Maass.
Summary: Text and photographs depict the typical activities of summer.
ISBN 0-8050-2087-X (alk. paper)
1. Summer—Juvenile literature.   [1. Summer.]   I. Title.   QB637.6.M3   1993   508—dc20   92-26955

First edition

and sun pours down...

that's when summer comes.

Early in summer the first fruits are ripe for eating.

Fresh-picked vegetables appear at roadside stands.

Fifers march
and fireworks flare

when the corn's knee-high
on the Fourth of July.

Water's best in summertime. Cool and clear,
it gushes from a sprinkler or tosses breezes at the beach

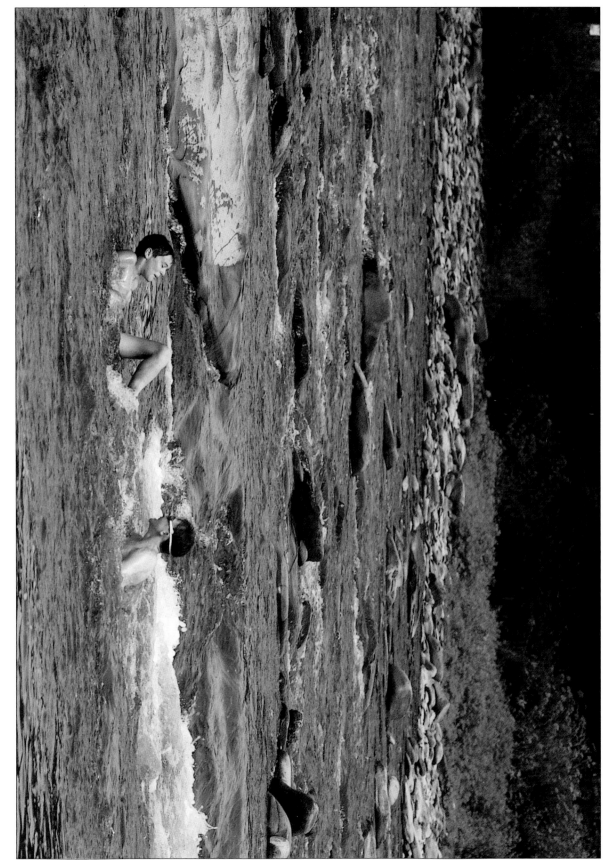

or swirls in a rushing stream.

It's also the place to catch fish.

Summer is a time
for street fairs
sandwiched between
city buildings.
The hot summer night is
filled with brassy music,
lights, and magic.

Country fairs under
bright summer skies
mean food and games and fun,
a place to show prize animals
(or take a break in the shade).

Baseball makes
summer dreams
come true.

When summer comes, a hot dog from the grill

or a slice of
juicy watermelon
is better than a fancy meal.

There's money
to be made,

and money to be spent.

Summer is a time for new experiences

and old-fashioned pleasures.

When the last stalks tower and the flowers are full-blown,

it's time to gather summer's late harvest.

There's one more swing to try, one more ride to take,

and one more day at the beach. Then, much too soon,
a cool breeze blows, and summer slips away.

It's hard to say good-bye to summer.

WITCHY THINGS is the winning text of the PREMIO NARRARE LA PARITÀ 2019 (NARRATING EQUALITY AWARD), which is celebrating its fifth edition.

The award was created by the Italian association Woman to Be to spread equality in literature, promote respect for identity and battle stereotypes.

NubeOcho publishes this year's winner in Spanish and English. Matilda Editrice publishes the book in Italian.

Witchy Things
Egalité Series

© Text: Mariasole Brusa, 2019
© Illustrations: Marta Sevilla, 2019
© Edition: NubeOcho, 2020
© Translation: Cecilia Ross, 2020
www.nubeocho.com · hello@nubeocho.com

Original title: *Turchina la strega*
Text Editing: Rebecca Packard

First edition: August 2020
ISBN: 978-84-17673-60-4
Legal Deposit: M-22504-2019

Printed in Portugal.

WITCHY THINGS

MARIASOLE BRUSA
MARTA SEVILLA

UH-OH!

What has happened to the WITCH'S CAULDRON?

What are those SCREAMS?

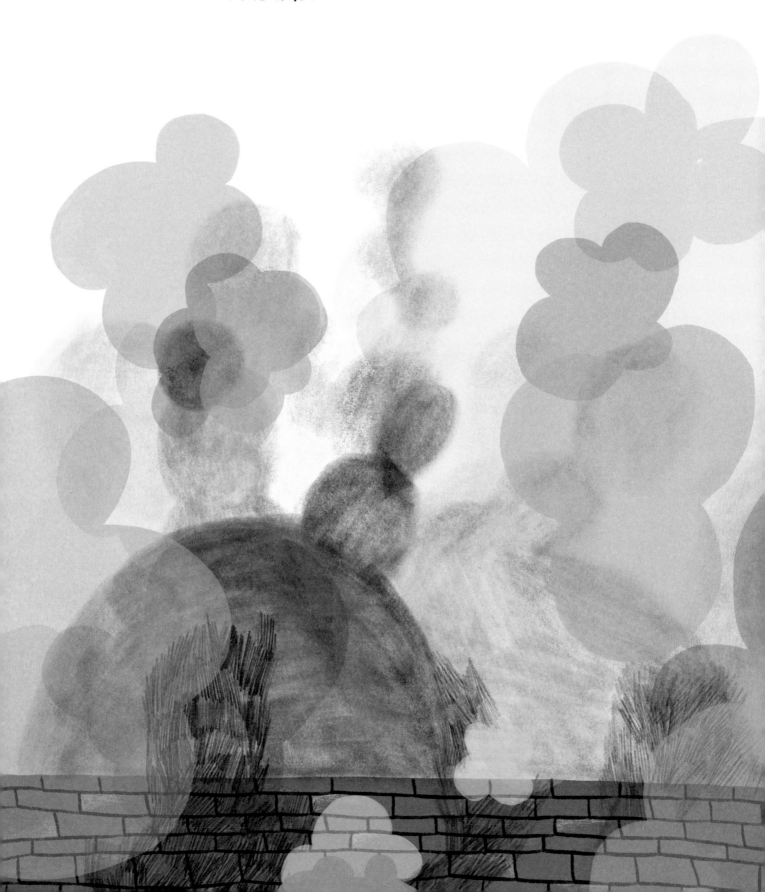

"Oh, for the love of STINKING SKUNK FARTS! This POTION doesn't work! My hair is still BLUE!"

If only the POTION
had turned my hair...

BLOOD RED,

OR ASH GREY,

or perhaps BOOGER GREEN.

But blue like THE BLUE FAIRY?
That sweet, smiling goody-goody?

BLECH!

The witch is in a bad mood but has a BRILLIANT IDEA.

"I have to prove that even though my hair is blue,
I'm still A REAL WITCH, a really BAD ONE.

I KNOW! I'll find A LITTLE KID to snatch!"

HEE, HEE, HEE, HEE!

The witch hides in the park and spies on ADAM, who is playing with SOME DOLLS. The witch smiles.

"This LITTLE BRAT will be perfect! He seems marvelously naughty, too—he's stolen those dolls so he can break them and make his sister angry... EXCELLENT!"

The witch jumps out from behind the bushes
and stands before Adam.

"Hee, hee, hee! I'm going to SNATCH YOU!"

"WHY?" asks Adam.

"What do you mean why?

Because I'm A WITCH!"

"So what if you're a witch?" asks ADAM.

"Well, witches SNATCH LITTLE KIDS," replies the witch.

"BUT WHY?"

"Because we're witches,
and we do WITCHY THINGS!"

"YEAH, BUT WHY?"

The witch is so angry she throws HER HAT
on the ground and stomps on it repeatedly.

"Because! Because, because, because!
Boys do boy things, like PESTERING their sisters,
and witches do witchy things, like SNATCHING LITTLE KIDS!"

"I don't PESTER my sister," says Adam.

"Oh, yeah?" sneers the witch. "Then what are you doing with those dolls?"

"Their HAIR," replies Adam. "The thing is, my dolls all have REALLY SHORT HAIR. But yours..."

Adam jumps up onto the witch's shoulders.

"Hmm... I'm thinking something WILD.
Some long ghastly BRAIDS, a nice bat bun..."

"Hey! Quit TUGGING! Ow!" the witch cries as she tries
to shoo him off, but the boy is lightning quick.

"For the love of stinking skunk farts! I'm going to pull out ALL YOUR NOSE HAIRS and make you EAT THEM!"

"I didn't know witches were so whiny," Adam teases.

"I'm not whining... OWWW!"

"DONE!" Adam exclaims.

The boy holds up a MIRROR for her to see. The witch has her hair up LIKE A TOWER and her braids look like SNAKES with tufts in all directions.

"MARVELOUS!

This is the MOST INCREDIBLE SORCERY I've ever seen!"

"You know?" says Adam. "Instead of doing witchy things to FEEL more like a witch, you could do THINGS YOU LIKE, just because you like them."

"Such as?" asks the witch.

"I don't know. I like doing hair. WHAT ABOUT YOU?"